Every Puppy

Born in Glasgow, Scotland, Eric Allan received his veterinary qualifications from the University of Melbourne, Australia. He is currently active in his Melbourne-based veterinary practice and is a member of the Royal College of Veterinary Surgeons.

Author of the best-selling books *Every Cat* and *Every Dog*, he has travelled extensively in the United States and worked in the United Kingdom.

By the same author:

Everydog (with Rowan Blogg)
Everycat (with Lynda Bonning)
Sally's New Puppy

Every Puppy

Perfect Pet or Perfect Pest?

Eric Allan

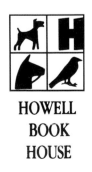

HOWELL
BOOK
HOUSE

First published in 1995 by
Hyland House Publishing Pty Limited, Australia

Copyright © 1995 text Eric Allan
              © 1995 cartoons Ian Bullock

Howell Book House
A Simon & Schuster Macmillan Company
1633 Broadway
New York, NY 10019

MACMILLAN is a registered trademark of Macmillan, Inc.

ISBN 0-87605-474-2
Library of Congress Cataloging-in-Publication Data

Allan, Eric.
    Every puppy: perfect pet or perfect pest? / Eric allan.
        p.   cm.
    ISBN 0-87605-474-2
    1. Puppies. I. Title.
SF427.A56   1996
636.7'07--dc20

Manufactured in Hong Kong

10 9 8 7 6 5 4 3 2 1

Contents

Acknowledgements

The author would like to thank Uncle Bens of Australia for their great assistance in providing many photographs, together with some of the information in the tables. Thanks also to Lesley Abbott for her excellent typing and Rose Kitching for assistance in editing the manuscript. Thanks also to Dr Robert Holmes for his help and expertise concerning dog behaviour.

Most of the photographs in this book are by Di Gatehouse, James Gatehouse and Sue Ward. The ones on pages 10, 15, 16, 23, 32, 41 and 43 are donated by Uncle Bens of Australia. The front cover photograph was kindly provided by Sebastian Costanzo.

Perfect pet or perfect pest!

Your puppy depends almost entirely on you. All its physical requirements like feeding, housing, worming and grooming are important. However, it is in the development of the pup's *character* that your role is crucial—here you can produce either a wonderful companion or a troublesome pest.

Two out of every ten person-dog relationships don't make it, although most could have. Often, this is not due to physical problems such as disease or accidents. The usual problem is unacceptable behaviour. Most puppy owners will be confronted with at least some behaviour problems and this book is designed to help solve them.

If you know what to look for and can confront any problems early, you will achieve good behaviour.

At the same time, this book will help you look after the pup's physical needs so it will enjoy good health.

Choosing the pup that is right for you

When choosing your puppy, the single most important factor is that its personality should be right for you. All other qualities, such as breed, size, coat colour, sex and cost become irrelevant if you don't actually like the dog. Ninety-nine per cent of owners grow to think of their dog as a member of the family. Most of us talk to our dog, are aware of its moods and think it is aware of ours. We take photos of it, share our snacks with it and generally allow it to be part of our lives. It is worth taking plenty of time to consider all of the options and responsibilities.

Remember, you are likely to have to live with the dog for the next ten to fifteen years. A dog can greatly enhance your quality of life. It is a shame that many pups, often bought on an

impulse, actually make life difficult for their owners. A dog that is to grow up with children must be especially carefully chosen. It must be trustworthy, not only with your own children but with visiting friends. An over-protective dog can be dangerous. If you choose carefully, you will be greatly rewarded.

What do you want from a dog?

Probably you would like your dog to be affectionate, obedient, reliable, responsible and a playful friend. Most dogs have the potential for all of this, but it can only be achieved through a suitable effort on your part. Selecting the right pup is obviously a good start.

Size

On the next page is a list of dogs arranged according to their weight. It is not all-inclusive but might give you a starting point in deciding

which dog is right for you. If you are thinking of getting one of the larger breeds, consider the following:

- How much room have you got?
- Will you be able to exercise the dog regularly?
- How much attention can you give/does the dog need?
- Can you afford to feed and maintain it?
- Can you control it?

Your home environment will determine whether you can have a large dog or not. Some breeds simply must have plenty of room if they are to be happy. All need somewhere to sleep, to eat and to exercise. In general, a small dog is more suitable for someone living in a flat or a house with little garden space. Small dogs eat less, produce less urine and fewer droppings (a bigger factor than you might anticipate!) and generally cost less to keep.

Even if you want a dog partly for protection, you don't necessarily need a large one.

Temperament

The temperament of your dog will depend a lot on its experiences as a small puppy. The way it has been handled, both by its mother

Toy dogs (under 5kg/11lb)	Small dogs (5—10kg/11—22lb)	Medium dogs (10—25 kg/22—55lb)
Australian silky	Australian terrier	Basenji
Chihuahua	Boston terrier	Basset hound
English toy terrier	Cairn terrier	Beagle
Italian greyhound	Cavalier King Charles	Bedlington
Maltese	King Charles spaniel	Blue heeler
Miniature pinscher	Lakeland terrier	Border collie
Miniature dachshund	Miniature schnauzer	Bull terrier
Papillon	Miniature poodle	Cocker spaniel
Pekinese	Pug	Hungarian puli
Pomeranian	Shih tzu	Keeshond
Toy poodle	Lhasa apso	Kelpie
Yorkshire terrier	Tibetan spaniel	Schnauzer
	West Highland white terrier	Scottish terrier
		Shetland sheepdog
		Springer spaniel
		Staffordshire bull terrier
		Standard poodle
		Welsh corgi
		Welsh terrier
		Whippet

Large dogs (25—40 kg/55—88lb)		Giant dogs (over 40 kg/over 88lb)
Afghan hound	German shepherd	Bloodhound
Airedale terrier	Golden retriever	Bull mastiff
Borzoi	Greyhound	Deerhound
Boxer	Hungarian vizsla	Giant schnauzer
British bulldog	Labrador	Great Dane
Chow chow	Old English sheepdog	Irish wolfhound
Dalmatian	Pointer	Mastiff
Doberman	Rhodesian ridgeback	Newfoundland
Foxhound	Samoyed	Rottweiler
German short-haired pointer	Scotch collie	St Bernard
	Setter	
	Weimaraner	

Note: Male dogs are usually slightly bigger than female dogs.

and the people caring for it, will mould its temperament as an adult.

Influence of the mother

Don't just look at the pups. Look at their parents, especially the mother. She must have a good temperament.

Russian silver fox breeders found that they could tame wild foxes by selecting parents which had stable temperaments and were tractable. It wasn't easy—in fact it took twelve generations. They then discovered they could do exactly the opposite in *one* generation.

The mother's influence on the puppy's temperament is enormous. This is partly because the pup inherits her disposition, but mainly it is her behaviour and attitude as a mother that moulds the pup's personality. A nervous, timid mother is likely to raise fearful pups that are much less liable to develop into suitable pets than those from a good mother.

For example, when the pup is four or five weeks old, its mother will start to walk away from it. The pup will naturally follow, but will be pushed away with growls and soft or 'inhibited' bites. If the mother is not self-controlled and gives a lot of bites that are too rough, the pup is likely to become timid.

Influence of people

It is also at this time that the pup should become used to socialising with people and being handled. Dogs in breeding kennels may not get as much of this as they should. Pups bred on 'puppy farms' are even less likely to receive this vital bonding early and at the time they are most receptive.

From four weeks on, puppies should be exposed to as many experiences and stimulations as possible. This should include meeting a variety of people and other kinds of dogs, and getting used to noises, music, lights and so on. This helps them, as adults, to cope better with similar experiences.

So, when you come to choose a pup, look at the way it has been bred and brought up. If it has been well-handled and

socialised and has a good mother, then these are all factors which are going to help you to develop it into a better pet.

Age

The best time to introduce a pup into your home is when it is **six to eight weeks old**. At this time the mother is trying to break her ties with it, so the pup is looking for someone to bond with and will form close attachments to you. This will make it easier for you to mould it into your way of life.

Some breeders and vets are reluctant to allow a pup out of the breeding kennels until it has been fully vaccinated at twelve to fourteen weeks. Certainly there are some risks involved in taking the puppy early, but these can be minimised with sensible precautions (that it mixes only with healthy vaccinated dogs and that it is kept away from places where other dogs toilet, especially trees and posts and places where dogs congregate, such as dog shows and parks). The benefits to the puppy's later behaviour of an early move far outweigh the risks.

A young pup is not suitable for everyone. Older people, for example, may not want to cope with its exuberance and the mess it is likely to create. Working couples may not have the time that a pup needs. If you cannot afford the time and patience needed to bring up a young pup properly, you should be honest with yourself and look for an adult dog.

Pups with short coats are better for warm or hot climates.

Type of coat

The type of coat a dog has is a big concern for some people. Long coats need lots of attention and, often, daily grooming. Do you have the time? Do you have the inclination? Old English sheep-dogs look utterly gorgeous as pups *but* they are going to grow up into thirty to forty kilograms of tangled mess unless you commit yourself to the care they need.

Shedding of coats is a consideration if the dog is to spend time inside. Most dogs lose *some* hair right through the year, and lose *a lot* in spring. Dogs who don't shed usually need regular clipping (take this into account when looking at what your dog will cost you).

If a dog is to live outside, choose a suitable breed. The heavy coated breeds such as samoyeds and huskies are not going to enjoy hot weather, but the short coats are less suitable for frosty or wet conditions. Be sensible about the dog's comfort and the climates for which various breeds were developed.

Cost

When you buy a puppy, you are committing yourself to the responsibility for its care. It is not just the initial cost you should consider, but also the ongoings. It is surprising how much it can all add up to, so do your sums before promising the family a particular breed of dog.

While the initial payment for a crossbreed might be small, you are still going to have high feeding bills if you have chosen one that is likely to grow into a large dog. Even small dogs can have a substantial impact on your weekly budget.

You must look after the dog. You will need to have it regularly vaccinated, wormed, probably neutered, and perhaps boarded at kennels when you are on holiday. Other costs may include registration, clipping and grooming and sundry veterinary fees.

If you cannot afford a dog, don't despair. There are lots of other pets that you can consider until you have more surplus cash.

Sex

There are no strictly male or female characteristics in dogs, especially if they have been neutered, although males do tend to be more territorial and self assertive than females.

Un-neutered females

If not neutered, a female will come into season about twice a year. This lasts about three weeks and there will be a moderate to copious vaginal discharge at this time. Male dogs will be strongly attracted and the female will also be keen to find a mate, especially in the middle week.

Un-neutered males

Un-neutered males can also develop nuisance sexual behaviour such as aggression, particularly with other male dogs, urine spraying or marking, often in other people's homes, roaming in search of a mate, mounting other pets and riding human legs. They are generally more active than neutered dogs and therefore more liable to have fights, car accidents and even trips to the pound.

Neutering

Both males and females can make excellent pets, but unless you are keen to breed it is best to have them neutered. Think of the ordeal an unwanted litter will cause. There are already too many unwanted dogs waiting for homes at animal welfare agencies. Thousands are euthanased each year.

Neutering is usually done at around six months of age for both males and females. It costs more to have a female done, but set against the overall cost of keeping a dog, this does not make much difference.

Pure breed or crossbreed?

If you choose a particular breed you know at least approximately how it will turn out. Both its physique and its characteristics will be similar to other members of the breed.

The major advantage of a crossbreed is that it is much more likely to be free of the diseases to which many breeds are prone. Crossbreeds are of course cheaper, and often they are stronger and more vigorous than some of the purebreds.

If you want a purebred pup, you should contact the breed society and discuss with the secretary or one of their members whether your choice is a good one. Obviously they will be enthusiastic about the dogs they breed, but many breeders are anxious for their puppies to go to a good home and they are in an excellent position to know if the breed will suit you. They can also provide you with a list of reliable breeders.

You are going to have your dog for ten to fifteen years or more. It is worth selecting very, very carefully.

Which breed suits you?

Pointer pups can be cuddled and carried but adults need lots of space.

When people decide to get a puppy they often have a *particular* breed in mind and become set on this. It is worth noting that for most people there are *many* breeds that would suit them. The

most important factor is still the individual dog's temperament and personality.

Do not be distracted by strings of show successes (unless you are going to become a serious breeder yourself). The odds are well against the perfect physical specimen also being the best adjusted pet. If I have a plea to breeders, it is to take this into account and to select for breeding only those dogs with a good temperament.

There are many other considerations. If you like walking and want your dog to join you then there are many breeds, such as setters and collies, that are suitable. Will you be taking your dog in the car, on holidays or even to work? Many tradespeople have a medium-sized dog such as a bull terrier or an Australian cattle dog to mind their tools while they are on site.

When you are selecting a breed, look at the characteristics of the adult, not the puppy.

Breeders: you and them

If you have decided on a particular breed or drawn up a short list, what then? How do you find a good breeder?

Directories of studs and breeders are available through various governing bodies like the Kennel Club and canine associations. Find their telephone numbers through the Yellow Pages or look them up in dog fanciers magazines.

Be careful! The majority of breeders are genuine. They love their dogs and won't sell to unsuitable homes. However, as in any group where there is money involved, there are unethical and dishonest individuals. They often put up a glossy front and advertise heavily. Be especially careful if the breed you have selected is currently popular.

Most breeders will check you out to ensure you will give their pup a good home. You shouldn't resent this, as they are looking after everyone's interests. They know how the dog will turn out, and if it is not the best choice for you it is better to find out now.

Some breeders encourage you to choose your puppy right away, so that you can visit regularly and share in the pup's development. I believe it is better to wait until the pup's personality is more apparent, so that each puppy can be best tailored to the most suitable owner.

Pet Shops: Buyer beware!

Pet shops can be excellent, but they can also be dreadful. Many are staffed by informed and conscientious people who are keen to find you a good pet, to keep it healthy and for you to be a satisfied customer. Unfortunately, though, others are not.

The origin of many of the animals sold through pet shops is *unknown* and so are their parent's characteristics. Some people will breed puppies just to supply pet shops, or will unload unwanted litters on them. These pups are rarely well-socialised and frequently have health and parasite problems.

Be careful if you buy from a shop. Get a guarantee so that if your purchase doesn't work out you can start again.

Other places to get pups

In every large town or city, there will be animal shelters, lost dogs' homes or welfare organisations. They can be a rich source of pets, although usually the dogs available are already mature. These dogs are in need of a home and will be euthanased unless they find one, so it is worth at least a phone call or a visit.

Can't find the right dog? Don't get desperate!

If you are finding it difficult to get the pup you want, try not to get desperate. Don't buy a pup for its looks, and certainly don't buy if the pup is wary or difficult to approach, or is smelly and ill-groomed or badly nourished. Some breeders offer the choice of a lot of pups, but if none have had the early love and care they need to make them into good pets, keep looking.

You'll never find out unless you have a good look!

Coming home and
settling in

The first few days in its new home can be overwhelming for the new pup. It will need rest, and time to explore and settle in without continual interference such as being picked up or carried constantly. Children in particular need to understand this.

At first, the pup has no idea where it is to sleep or eat and it is certainly going to be unreliable when it comes to toilet time (see House training, page 28).

Let the pup wander around its new territory while you supervise. When it is left alone you should restrict the space available to it. You can meet all its needs by giving it enough room to eat, sleep and toilet, plus a bit more just to investigate and play in.

Later on, when it's a bit more reliable and predictable, you can relax a little, although for some time it will probably consider anywhere outside its den as a good place to go to the toilet. It will try to avoid going until it can get outside its own den, but its idea of 'outside' will include your lounge and dining room!

Show the pup its bed as soon as it has finished its first exploration. This should be in a quiet, warm and draught-free area.

Even if your dog is eventually going to sleep outside, it might be wise to have it indoors for the first few nights.

Pups need lots of sleep so allow it *undisturbed* rest. For the first night or two, most pups will whimper or cry loudly and continually. Food and toys have little effect. It is comfort and contact they want. Don't rush in and overdo the comforting or you will prolong the settling-in period. You may find that a softly playing radio, or a loudly ticking alarm clock will help. More likely, an old pyjama jacket or T-shirt of yours, wrapped over a hot water bottle and tucked in beside the pup will ease it through the night.

Have clean water available at all times, but only give the pup food at meal times. Suitable dishes are ones that cannot be knocked over easily, chewed up or dragged around. Consider a ceramic bowl.

The cotton wool syndrome: unwrap your pup

In its first days with you, your puppy should be exposed to lots of experiences, stimulations and even stresses. It is a mistake to be

over-protective and to shield it
from normality. Walk around,
don't tiptoe. Pups need to experience different people and animals, stresses like the vacuum
cleaner, loud noises, windy days
or whatever else they are going
to face later. Pups that are pro-
tected from stresses early *do not
cope nearly as well later.*

Similarly, pups that don't
meet with other dogs before they are four months old are likely to
react fearfully and badly when they do.

The young pup has a very receptive mind. It is like a dry sponge
that absorbs new information rapidly. At six weeks of age, however, it probably hasn't learned much about *fear*. This is why
exposure to potentially stressful experiences is better now than
later on when it will find them harder to accept. Let your pup be
touched and fondled, squeezed a little and shown to friends and
neighbours. Take it with you to the beach (if this is permitted), on
the train and get it used to noisy traffic. Try to introduce it to *all*
the sights and sounds it will experience as an adult.

Mixing with other pets

Most adult dogs do not consider a young pup as much of a rival,
other than for your attention. Nevertheless, watch carefully. The
new puppy is a stranger in the household and might be seen as a
threat or a possible enemy. It is a good idea to have a lead on the
adult dog and be prepared to step in if you have to.

If the adult dog is particularly territorial, it is a good idea to
take it with you to meet the new pup on *neutral* ground such as a
park. At home, your dog will be guarding its possessions, food and
sleeping place, so a meeting in the park will ensure that it is less
guarded and protective.

After a few days, however, you will have to allow a natural
pecking order to develop. The adult dog will discipline an unruly
pup's behaviour in its own way. If the dog is not too aggressive,
this hierarchy should be allowed to develop.

Cats are a greater risk. They are liable to lash out at over-
exuberant pups, so scratch wounds and eye injuries are possible.
Allow the cat plenty of room to escape and don't allow the pup to
persistently harass it.

Discipline

Pups that are not disciplined when young are almost impossible to train later. Discipline doesn't mean hitting the dog. It means clearly and consistently letting the dog know what it can't do. Simply do not allow behaviour that you will not accept later. This goes for mouthing and biting, jumping up, stealing food, destroying furniture and so on.

Dogs have an innate desire to please and an affinity for human company. Nevertheless, you have to earn and maintain their respect. They *will* try you out to see if they can dominate you. This is as natural for them as eating and sleeping. Read Establishing good behaviour (pages 58-71). It will be well worth your while.

Understanding the pup's mind: *nose* more than it *knows*!
When you are walking in the park with your dog, you may not realise that the sensations it is experiencing are very different from yours. Your primary sense is *sight* (but you also hear and smell a little and will be aware of movement, such as the breeze, and touch, such as the softness of the grass). Your dog, however, is bombarded by *scents and sensations* (of sound and movement) and

bombarded by *scents and sensations* (of sound and movement) and relies much less than you on its eyes.

As well as this, your dog has no concept of time. We can enjoy and appreciate the peacefulness of the park but also be planning to get home in time for lunch. For dogs, things are much simpler. Their thoughts are only of the *moment*. They cannot think logically, nor can they anticipate anything beyond the immediate effect of their actions.

Dogs may be highly intelligent, but they cannot reason. They do very little conscious thinking, despite what Walt Disney and Warner Brothers suggest. Most of their behaviour is learned response. It is easy to overestimate your puppy's ability and attribute to it a sense of logic that it doesn't have. Simple cause and effect links make up the vast majority of its responses. It learns by association, so the fastest and most effective way to train a puppy is to reward it every time it gets something *right*.

Reward good deeds

Left above: To a hound, heaven is an earthy smell.

Left below: A little exploratory digging is normal and doesn't warrant punishment.

Positive reward by praise, patting or even a small titbit of food is far more effective than the punishment of misdeeds. Better for it to associate good deeds with rewards, and so to try for those, than for it to be in fear of pain or discomfort should it make a mistake. Some punishment is essential, but it need not be overly painful— just as long as the message is clear and delivered immediately, preferably within a single second and not longer than five seconds. Any time after this is too late.

After a while it is no longer necessary to reward your puppy every time it does what you want. It has been shown with human gamblers that intermittent reward is far more likely to result in addiction than either always or never winning. **It would be nice to have your pup addicted to good behaviour.**

How your puppy reads you: being consistent

Dogs do not see with the colours and clarity of focus that we enjoy, but they are still very good at reading our body language— not just physical movement and stance, but our body chemistry as well. The spoken word is of limited use to them, although many dogs can ultimately learn to recognise fifty or more individual words.

So, when training or instructing your puppy, your *actions and attitude* are more important than the command itself. It is extremely perceptive of your moods and the subtle nuances of your posture. If you give a command, you have to mean it. If you lack the right tone or conviction, your command is ineffectual. To the dog it's not just *what* you say, but *how* you say it. It understands your body language and tone of voice far more accurately than your vocabulary.

Your puppy's moods
Dogs react in simpler and more predictable ways than people, but their responses too will vary with the time and place and their mood at that moment. If a dog is highly aroused or fearful, then an aggressive reaction is more likely than if it were calm. There is a constant, fluid interplay between its automatic, instinctive reactions and its learned responses. The environment at the time has quite a lot to do with how the dog ultimately reacts.

If your pup is very excited or already distracted, then it is unlikely to be obedient or responsive. You can't expect too much at these times. Punishment for misbehaviour such as not returning to your call, or even urinating on the carpet whilst in a boisterous state, is probably neither very fair nor very productive.

Don't try to teach your puppy if it is too excited. Wait until it has settled down.

House training (toilet training)

Pups need to pass urine and faeces quite often. Getting them to do this in an acceptable area can take a little time and patience.

You must first decide whether you want to train your pup to use paper or if you want it housebroken. If someone will be at home to observe the pup and can get it to a suitable outside toilet area fast, then go for housebreaking. Otherwise, start with paper-training.

Paper-training
Pups will avoid soiling in their eating or sleeping areas if they can. They will move away, sometimes only a few feet but sometimes much further. Some pups rapidly develop a preference for a specific area to eliminate in, while others form a liking for a type of *surface*, such as lino, wood or carpet, grass or dirt.

At first, put papers over most of the room. If the pup does show a preference for one area then

you can remove the paper from the rest of the room. The pup will gradually associate paper with toileting and you can slowly move the paper to an area that suits you. This may need to be done by only a hand's-breadth a day for some pups. Others will happily just look for the paper and oblige.

Housebreaking

Pups usually need to go to the toilet soon after eating, after waking up and when they are excited or after play or vigorous exercise. If you are lucky, the pup may give you a warning by displaying preparatory signs such as sniffing, walking in circles or heading off towards a preferred area (its, not yours). Pups will try to get out of the place they consider to be their 'den' before toileting. Unfortunately, they do not consider the entire house as their den and will actively try to get into some other room, such as the dining room or lounge, before urinating or worse.

So, select an appropriate toilet area and take the pup to it at the times that it is likely to eliminate or when it shows signs of needing to go. Praise and stroke the pup as a reward when it gets it right. This is powerful reinforcement.

Be patient with your puppy as it learns (and inevitably makes mistakes). Aversive or frightening techniques such as shouting or rubbing the pup's nose in the mess are likely to confuse and frighten it and to prolong the housebreaking period.

If you notice the pup in the act of soiling in the wrong spot within five seconds (no more), then say **'no!'** and pick it up and take it immediately to the preferred spot.

Sometimes the pup will refuse your selected area. This can be for a variety of reasons. It may not like the surface—some prefer grass to soil, others don't like to be under trees because the noise and movement intimidates them. Rain, hail and wind can adversely affect them. You need to maintain your patience and restrain yourself if the pup gets it wrong. Try to work out its preferences by allowing the pup to choose for itself a few times then find a similar area or surface that is mutually acceptable.

Excited puppies make mistakes

Pups will urinate sometimes when they are excited or when you greet them and pat them. Urinating, especially if associated with the posture of crouching down with ears held flat and back and eyes wide, may be 'submissive' behaviour—a sign of accepting your dominant status. Pups should not be punished for this. They usually outgrow it, but you may have to avoid getting these pups excessively excited while they are in the house.

Cleaning up the mess

When cleaning up the mess, use water and mild detergents, not cleaners with strong odours, and particularly avoid ammonia-based products. These seem to encourage pups to return to the same spot. It is better if the pup does not witness you doing the cleaning up. This seems to reinforce its interest in that particular area.

If the pup fouls in the street, or in some public place, do the right thing and clean it up. This is good manners, good public relations and, in some places, it is also the law.

A toilet trained pup is far more socially acceptable.

Feeding

Giving your pup the right food need not be a difficult or complicated task. However, there are some traps you might fall into so it is well worth reading the whole of this section. A correct diet will reward you with a healthy pup, well set up for later life.

Food to start your pup off on

Try to find out what the pup is used to being fed. The breeder, pet shop or animal shelter may have provided you with a diet sheet. Start off by feeding it similar food and make any changes gradually. The pup has a lot of adjustments to achieve in its new home, so easing in any change of diet helps it settle down more quickly.

The right stuff

In a good puppy diet, **meat alone is not enough**. Undomesticated carnivores eat the whole of their prey, including the bones, internal organs and gut contents. They also eat a certain amount of vegetable matter, fruits and berries.

A suitable diet for pups must:

- Be tasty and easily digested.
- Be high in **protein** and **carbohydrates** (to make them grow and give them energy).
- Contain all the essential nutrients at appropriate levels.

It doesn't matter if every spoonful doesn't have exactly the right balance of nutrients, vitamins and calories. It's the overall balance that counts. Puppies' digestive systems are very adaptable and, within limits, can tolerate excesses. However, absolute *deficiencies* of essential nutrients will make the whole diet inadequate. Pups develop and grow rapidly, so even small deficiencies can lead to problems.

Commercial diets

There are some excellent commercial puppy foods available, satisfying all the pup's nutritional requirements. No supplementary vitamins and minerals are necessary if the product is clearly labelled as being '**complete and balanced**'. Ask your vet to recommend a specific product.

A drawback to commercial foods, especially canned products, is that they do not provide enough exercise for the pup's teeth and gums. This problem can be overcome by giving your puppy a raw bone several times a week. Commercial foods are also highly palatable and high in calories, so beware of overfeeding.

Home diets

If you decide to make up your own diet, make sure you include a selection of all of the following food groups:

Meat

Puppies can eat meat raw or cooked, although if there is any doubt as to the source of the meat it is safer to cook it. When the pup is older, cut the meat into larger strips or chunks to encourage chewing and proper development of the teeth, gums and jaw structures.

Raw meat does *not* make dogs savage, although it is so attractive to other dogs that it might be worth fighting over.

Vegetables

Dogs cannot digest plant fibre, so raw vegetables, even if diced or grated, have limited worth as a source of nutrition. Cooked vegetables, however, form an excellent and important part of your pup's diet that can easily be digested. Try to get it used to vegetables right from the start so it will accept and enjoy them in adult life.

Carbohydrates (includes cereals, bread, pasta and potatoes)

Carbohydrates are essential for a growing pup as they provide energy. They are rapidly digested and converted to glucose, the body's fuel.

Bones

Surprisingly, cooking bones makes them less digestible. It also makes them more likely to splinter into sharp dangerous shards. Raw bones, on the other hand, provide the pup with excellent oral exercise, are good for their teeth and are great as boredom beaters and tension terminators. However, dogs do have a drive to bury bones and this can be frustrating for keen gardeners.

Fat

A certain amount of fat should be left on the meat and bones that you feed your puppy. It is a good energy source and, in moderation, is tolerated well by dogs. You need not worry about cholesterol problems and hardened arteries—dogs don't suffer from them.

Eggs

Eggs are a great source of high quality, very digestible protein. However, the raw whites contain 'avidin' which, over a long period, could cause a vitamin B (Biotin) deficiency. Light cooking destroys the avidin and also improves digestibility.

Scraps

In general, scraps are a useful and helpful addition to the diet, but do be discriminating. Do not overload the pup with large amounts of food it is not used to, such as curries, pasta sauces and pork crackling. If you do give it scraps, remember to adjust the amount of other food you give, otherwise your puppy will get fat.

Don't forget to remove any cooked bones from your scraps before feeding them to the puppy.

Supplements

The use of supplements is a controversial issue. In the past, when many commercial diets were inadequate and lacked sufficient calcium and some vitamins, the addition of these ingredients made some sense. However, commercial food has improved dramatically in the last ten to fifteen years so that very few good quality diets need supplementing. There is a real danger of adding *too much* to your dog's food.

Many breeders have evolved quite complex diet recommendations, mainly through a trial and error basis. They have found that adding things like kelp, brewer's yeast, garlic, calcium and so on have helped some dogs. Supplements can be beneficial for some dogs in certain situations but, overall, far simpler diets are just as nutritious. Many breeders will recommend excessive and dangerous levels of supplements which are also very expensive.

ENERGY REQUIREMENTS OF DOGS IN KCAL*/DOG/DAY

Age in months	Toy, e.g. Yorkshire terrier	Small, e.g. West Highland white terrier	Medium, e.g. Cocker spaniel	Large, e.g. Labrador	Giant, e.g. Great Dane
2-4	220-310	310-685	685-925	925-1850	1850-2775
4-6	310-465	465-685	925-1320	1850-2775	3700-4625

*Kcal is a measure of the energy content of food. The Kcal content of commercial foods is either stated on the label or is available on request. Individual products vary considerably, so check the package.

The careless use of supplements can be seriously detrimental to your dog's health, especially if given over long periods.

Here are two examples:
- Too much **calcium** interferes with other nutrients, such as **zinc** and **magnesium**, and can produce painful bone deformities.
- **Vitamin A** and **Vitamin D** are cumulative poisons. (One teaspoonful of Cod Liver Oil contains all the daily requirements of Vitamins A and D for a 50 kilogram/7-8 stone dog.) Over a period of time, the excess vitamins can build up to dangerously toxic levels, causing reduced appetite, weight loss, leg pain and hardening of tissues such as the lungs, kidney and stomach. Beef liver is a source of both Vitamins A and D and can lead to poisoning if given in excess.

How much should you feed?

The amount of food needed by puppies varies enormously. The chart on page 34 is **a guide only**. Individual puppies will need up to 25 per cent *more* or *less* than this. Some factors that change the amount required include the environmental temperature, whether the pup is housed inside or out, how much exercise it gets, how well it digests the food, its state of health and so on.

- Most **canned foods** contain 80-100 Kcal per hundred grams of food.
- **Dry foods** have around 300 Kcal per hundred grams.

First you dig it up, then you eat it!

How often should you feed?

Divide this daily ration into at least four meals until the pup is ten weeks old. Gradually reduce the frequency to twice daily. For most dogs up to medium size this should be done by the time the puppy is six months old. When the dog has reached maturity you can choose to reduce its mealtimes to one a day if you like.

Should food be warmed?

Dogs prefer their food to be at about blood temperature. The aroma of warm food can increase its appeal, but beware of giving food that is too hot as many pups will indiscriminately gulp it down, only to regret this too late to avoid burning the mouth and throat.

A simple way to heat the dog's food if you have just pulled it out of the fridge is to stir in some hot water.

Obesity: roly-poly puppy syndrome

Beware of producing a fat pup. An obese pup will almost always have weight problems as an adult.

You do *not* want the pup to grow at its maximum rate, especially if it is a breed that will mature at over thirty kilograms. It is better to allow the dog to grow at a *gradual* pace. Dogs that grow too fast are likely to develop disorders of their bones or joints that can result in lameness and pain and may eventually require surgery. Sometimes the damage is permanent.

Fat in pups is deposited in different places to people. You won't see a bulging waistline or flabby thighs in a dog. Instead, look in the area between the hind legs. There should be no 'udder-like' deposits of fat. Also feel over the ribcage. You should feel the ribs clearly beneath the skin—and not through a thick layer of fat.

If the pup is overweight but hungry, try adding lots of cooked vegetables and bran to the diet instead of calorie-rich food.

Fussy eaters

Dogs don't really know what is best for them, but they do know what they like. Most will try to manipulate your choice of food. When your puppy first arrives, and later on when it has little upsets like

teething, its appetite may be poor. Only particularly attractive foods will be tempting. Some puppies quickly realise that if they wait long enough, something better will come. Others are just not good eaters.

Do not fall into the trap of pandering to fussy eaters. They will not starve if they miss a few meals. Train your dog to eat in one area only and from its bowl only. Make sure it knows that the first food offered is all it's going to get. If it doesn't eat the food within fifteen minutes, take it away. Don't offer more until the next mealtime. Be consistent and persistent. You will win.

Water

Plenty of fresh, clean water should always be available. Dogs vary in their requirements but, unlike with food, are excellent at self regulation. Simply provide plenty and don't worry if they don't drink it, as long as they are healthy and active. Some pups get enough water in their food and require little more than that.

Milk

Giving your dog milk is a more controversial issue. Nature has designed the pup to come *off* its mother's milk at about four or five weeks of age and on to other food. Just how sensible is it, therefore, to put it back on to cow's milk?

Certainly, milk is *not* an essential component of a pup's diet. It is undoubtedly very nutritious, containing some useful minerals (especially calcium), vitamins, fats and protein, so if you want to give the pup milk that is okay, but be careful not to give too much at first. **The most common cause of diarrhoea in pups is milk, either due to an inability to properly digest it or simply because it has drunk too much.**

Start the pup on milk diluted with water. If this does not cause upsets, then you may *gradually* increase the amount given and make it less dilute. If the pup develops diarrhoea whenever it is given milk, simply don't give any more. It is a useful, but not essential, dietary component.

Some common questions

Are baby foods suitable?
Baby foods are expensive, have an incorrect balance and absolute insufficiency of nutrients for a pup's needs. They are for babies!

Is chocolate okay?
In moderation, and sometimes as a reward, chocolate or other highly palatable and sugary products are not harmful. However, be very careful. Pups can easily become very fond of these treats and you can create a problem for yourself whenever they are around. Chocolate in large amounts is **toxic** and can even be fatal. For example, half a block of cooking chocolate could kill a medium-sized dog.

Is cat food okay for dogs?
Yes, but it is very high in calories, and the cat may not agree...

Do garlic and onion prevent fleas?
For some dogs, the addition of a clove of garlic to the diet several times a week seems to prevent flea attacks. It does not work for all dogs and overdosage can be dangerous. Onion is similar and excess can produce a form of anaemia. Be moderate!

Does feeding rice stop the urine burning the lawn?
It might. In general, increasing carbohydrates such as rice and potato and reducing protein will help to avoid strong acid-urine production.

General care

Bathing

A dog's skin is very different from ours. Under all that hair, dog skin is relatively delicate. It is only one-third as thick as ours, has fewer glands, is less oily and has an **alkaline** pH level in contrast to our **acid** skin.

Most dogs do not need frequent bathing. Dogs don't sweat as humans do so most dirt and debris can be brushed or combed off. Talcum powder can be useful in removing debris or excessive skin oils. Simply brush it in against the lie of the coat then brush it out again.

As a general rule, do not bath the pup more than once a week. Soaps and shampoos designed for people are often too harsh for a pup's skin, so should be avoided. Obtain a product designed specifically for dogs, or a pure soap free from perfumes or other cosmetic additives. (Baby shampoos are tolerated well by most dogs.) This is especially important if it is necessary to bath the pup regularly as

too much exposure to harsh shampoos is likely to cause dermatitis.

Wash the pup gently and talk to it calmly and quietly as you go. Use warm water and select a place where there are no draughts. When washing the face, do only one side at a time. Lather up and rinse, then do the other side. This allows the pup to keep at least one eye open at a time and reduces potential anxiety.

Rinse all soap and shampoo from the skin and towel the pup dry. The depths of the coat will be difficult to dry using a towel and are likely to stay damp for longer. To dry thoroughly, give the pup a good brisk run or some other form of exercise or put it into a warm, draught-free area. Pups can get ill from becoming cold when they are still wet.

Beware!
Wet pups will be on the lookout for dirt to roll in, so don't just let them out into the garden. Dogs actually like to smell strongly, which is why they roll in things like fertiliser or dead birds. This may be socially revolting to us, but it's normal for the dog.

Choose the right size bath
It pays to start bathing a puppy in the way you want to bath it as an adult. For example, a small pup can get used to the sink, or a pup which will grow into a large dog can get used to the bath.

Grooming
Grooming, especially of the long-coated breeds, is a task which can be a pleasure or a chore. It is very much in your interest for the pup to enjoy grooming sessions. If your pup is a breed that requires regular, even daily, grooming, it is absolutely essential that you have a cooperative dog.

Use a brush or comb that is suited to your dog's hair type. Get advice on selection from an experienced dog groomer, such as a breeder, or from a professional at a dog grooming parlour, *not a pet shop*. Be prepared to buy good quality products, as cheap ones tend to damage the skin, especially in the young pup.

Talk to the pup in a calm even voice as you work. Brush the coat vigorously, parting long hair down to the skin. Some breeds have an undercoat plus a longer coat over the top. The undercoat is generally shed once a year, usually in spring or summer. This coat comes out in tufts and lumps and can make the dog itchy and irritable. It should be combed out—a brush is ineffective. A steel comb is preferable to a plastic one, which is rarely strong enough for the task.

Sensitive areas
Some dogs are sensitive about their paws, the inside of their legs and their underbelly. If

your pup is like this, brush a few strokes at a time in the sensitive area, then brush elsewhere. Return *intermittently* to the problem area rather than spending a long session on it and making the dog anxious or upset.

Matted hair

Matted hair is a problem that can be prevented by regular grooming. Once matts have formed, try the following approach: tease the matt apart, using a comb and some scissors. Clip the hair away at the base of the matt, but be extremely careful not to cut the skin. Use a pair of curved nail scissors if you have them. For severely matted coats you may need the services of a professional who will use electric clippers to remove the matt from just above the skin surface.

Start as you mean to go on

If you plan to use a grooming table when the pup gets older, it is a good idea to get it used to one as a pup.

Ears

In general, the ears should be left alone if possible, other than to get the pup used to you handling and inspecting them. Dogs can become very sensitive about their ears, and it is useful to gain their confidence when the ear is not painful or inflamed. This is especially true for breeds prone to ear problems, such as spaniels, poodles and any other breed with narrow or hairy canals or drooping ears.

Dogs that have hair growing in the canal should have it plucked out. This hair is not firmly rooted and can be painlessly removed if you do it regularly. Remove only a few hairs at a time by simply grasping them between thumb and forefinger and pulling. Your vet, a groomer or a breeder will give you a practical demonstration if you ask.

Ear problems

If your pup is showing any signs of discomfort with its ears, have them checked by your vet.

Signs that might indicate ear trouble include:

- Vigorous shaking of the head.
- Scratching at the ear base.
- A discharge or smell from the ear.
- Head tilted to one side.

Removing wax

If your pup tends to have waxy ears, regular removal of this wax will reduce the chances of infection developing. An ear full of wax is a wonderful opportunity for fungal or yeast infection to develop.

It is best to use a product designed specifically for this task, which can be obtained from your vet. You could also use a few drops of warm mineral oil, baby oil, or a preparation designed for use by people.

The dog's ear canal is long and deep. Do not probe in it with cotton buds, or you risk packing the wax deep into this canal. Use the ear drops or oil to soften the wax, wait ten to fifteen minutes, and then swab out with a piece of damp cotton wool wrapped around and covering your finger.

Teeth

Good dental habits established early on can ensure your dog a life free from dental disease and the build up of plaque and tartar. Dogs rarely develop cavities like people do, but they can suffer from a variety of gum and root diseases if their teeth are neglected.

Dogs have two sets of teeth. The **temporary** 'milk' teeth will start to emerge by the time the puppy is three or four weeks old. By the time it is six weeks old most of the twenty-eight baby teeth will have broken through.

The second set are **permanent** and will last for the rest of the dog's life. They usually start to come through when the puppy is between four and six months old.

- Incisors usually erupt at 4 to 5 months.
- Molars usually erupt at 4 to 7 months.
- Canines usually erupt at 5 to 6 months.

Teething

Teething rarely worries puppies. There may be occasional periods when they are reluctant to chew, drool more than usual and/or are very tired. Don't worry too much as this usually lasts for only a few hours and, at the most, a day.

However, your pup's teething may worry *you*. It will be more than ever keen to chew the furniture, plants, clothes, and anything else it can find. Make sure it has lots of legitimate chewing objects at this time (see Mouthing and biting, page 64).

Teething problems

Sometimes, the pup's temporary teeth may not be properly displaced by its permanent ones and will interfere and cause problems. This is most common with the canine teeth and your vet may have to remove any retained teeth. However, if you can induce the pup to chew vigorously on something like a meaty raw marrow bone, the problem can often be solved naturally.

Exercise

A normal pup has a lot of energy to burn. Your aim is to channel this into acceptable activities and therefore to minimise destructive behaviour, such as digging holes, pulling washing off the line and chewing up the furniture.

Don't overdo it!
Your pup's bones are soft and easily damaged. As they mature they will harden but in the meantime you must be careful. The joints are especially vulnerable to injury if stressed excessively. Avoid long runs and hard work up hills and over obstacles, *especially* if your pup is one of the larger breeds and *definitely* if the pup is overweight.

Running free
Walking your puppy on a lead is great for both of you (see below), but it *must* also be allowed some free, unfettered play where it can wander, explore and run or roll about as it pleases. If your garden is not large enough, look for a hazard-free area. (Pups are likely to run straight out on to roads, and an excited pup is unlikely to respond to your commands to stop.)

Being responsible
You are required by law to be in control of your dog. In some areas it is illegal for dogs to be off the lead. This is usually to ensure that other people and their pets are not inconvenienced and to protect native animals and wildlife. These are fair and reasonable aims, so obey the spirit of the law. However, try to find a safe area where the pup won't get into too much mischief, then let it have its freedom.

Be aware that a dog can upset a lot of people in a very short time and then all dog lovers suffer the consequences. A barking dog can be heard by hundreds of households and few will tolerate it, especially if it is loud and persistent or late at night.

In summary, observe a few golden rules:
- Keep your dog under control at all times—on the street, in public areas, in national parks and bushland.
- Clean up any mess the dog leaves behind.
- Not everyone likes dogs so respect the right of others to be left in peace.
- House pets are not *more* important than wild animals. Respect them all.

Fleas

The most common external parasite that is likely to affect dogs is, by far, the flea. Early recognition and treatment of fleas is important because they reproduce and spread at a phenomenal rate. For example, if as few as **ten** female fleas are allowed to breed they can produce over **a quarter of a million** eggs and larvae in a single month, *plus* around **two thousand adult fleas**.

Signs of flea infestation

Fleas are small parasites that feed by sucking blood from the dog's skin. They are fast moving and shy of light, so they can be difficult to see. Instead of looking for the adult fleas themselves, look for evidence of their presence. Flea 'dirt' or flea droppings are small dark crusty specks that can be seen on the dog's skin if you part the pup's coat and look closely.

Fleas like to feed around the tail base in the area between the hind legs and sometimes around the head and neck. Look in these areas for tell-tale droppings. If you are not sure, pick up some of the suspect skin debris, put it on some white paper and add a mild detergent solution. Flea 'dirt' will dissolve into a bloody-coloured stain.

Most of the problems caused by fleas are exaggerated by the pup's response to the intense irritation a bite produces. The pup will scratch, rub and bite at its skin, causing even more inflammation and irritation. The resulting itch–scratch vicious cycle is the most common skin complaint seen by vets. Early recognition and treatment can prevent painful skin complaints and unnecessary veterinary fees.

Treatment

There are many products available to control fleas, all useful in different ways and meeting different needs. Use one product or another, not a combination of insecticides as this will reduce their overall effectiveness. If you are unsuccessful in controlling the fleas, **do** consult your vet.

Powders

Flea powders are fairly safe and effective, but have only short-term action (most last only one to three days). They are useful though because they are easy to apply.

Apply by rubbing or brushing in against the lie of the coat. For pups it is advisable to wipe the coat with a damp towel or cloth after applying the powder. This removes any excess powder before the pup has a chance to lick it off.

Rinses
There are many types of rinses available and all are generally more effective than powder. They last longer and penetrate deeper, but may also be more toxic. Many of the insecticides used in the rinses are either potentially dangerous, or are ineffective due to a build-up of resistance by the fleas. Ask your vet to recommend a particular rinse. He or she will know which ones are best suited to your individual puppy.

Sprays
Some flea treatments are available in spray form or in pressure packs, but pups rarely like or tolerate these. They are better kept for the treatment of bedding or infested areas.

Flea collars
Flea collars have some effect on fleas, although as a sole weapon they are unreliable. They are not recommended for pups under twelve weeks of age.

Oral
There are two types of oral treatment. Both can be very useful in certain situations, for example, if the pup swims a lot.

One type of oral treatment contains a drug called an *insect growth regulator*. This makes the flea infertile. This type of drug is highly effective and low in toxicity but, at the moment, still expensive. It is given **once a month** mixed in the pup's food.

Other oral treatments contain an *insecticide*. These either enter the bloodstream and kill the flea when it bites, or act on the skin to kill and/or repel fleas. These are usually given **twice a week or more**.

Foggers or 'bombs'
These products contain ingredients that prevent eggs from hatching as well as killing any adult fleas present. They produce a fine mist which spreads widely and evenly over the target area. The active ingredients are low in toxicity and have a very narrow spectrum of activity, which means they have a minimal effect on anything other than fleas. They can be extremely effective, especially where the dog is kept within a confined area such as a flat or apartment.

The pup's environment
In treating fleas you should not only be aiming to kill the adults, you should also try to clean or clear the environment of eggs and

larvae. When you treat the pup with a rinse or powder, also provide clean bedding and vacuum the surrounds (bag and eliminate the sweepings), paying special attention to cracks, crevices and other dusty areas.

Worming

All pups should be 'wormed'. This means treating them against possible infection by the parasites that live inside their bodies. Worms can seriously affect a pup's health. Some are also potentially a danger to people.

There are two kinds of worms that must be treated: **intestinal worms** (roundworm, hookworm, whipworm and tapeworm) and **heartworm** (these live in the heart and major blood vessels supplying the lungs).

Intestinal worms

Treat all pups at least four times for all four types of intestinal worms.

There are four distinctly different types of intestinal worms. Their effects and the drugs needed to control them are also different. **A minimum course, using an 'all wormer' preparation, should be given when the pup is around six, eight, eleven and fourteen weeks old.** Ask your vet for information about worm infections in your area, as you may need frequent follow-ups, especially if hydatids or hookworm are endemic there. Intestinal worms can be diagnosed by an examination in the laboratory of the pup's droppings.

Roundworm
These are large worms that can reach the length of a pencil. The pup can be infected even before it is born, and massive infestations are possible. Because it is such a common infection and may be a health hazard for people (see below), it is routine to treat roundworm anyway, without necessarily getting a diagnosis first.

Signs
The worm larvae can cause damage to the lungs and liver as they migrate through the body. Adult worms live in the bowel and an affected pup is likely to be in poor condition, probably pot bellied and emaciated.

Infection of people
Roundworms pass enormous numbers of eggs. People picking these up can be affected as the larvae hatch and migrate through their bodies. The liver is the main site of damage but other organs including the eye can be infected.

The major risk is to children, especially the dirt-eating toddlers of two to four years old, so make sure children wash their hands after handling pups. All droppings should be removed as soon as possible.

Treatment
The drugs used against roundworm are safe and effective. If you own the pup's mother she must also be treated. Treatment *can* start when the pup is two weeks old, but pups generally don't come to your home until they are six weeks old.

After the first four treatments, if any roundworms are passed continue to treat every three weeks until you have two 'clear' treatments, that is no dead worms are passed. Continue to treat the pup/dog regularly (**every three to six months**) for the rest of its life.

Note
Roundworm treatment will also kill hookworm.

Hookworm
There are several types of hookworm, depending on the climate in which you live.

Signs
Hookworms are common and can seriously inflame the dog's bowel. Because they are bloodsuckers, they can also cause anaemia, weakness, diarrhoea and bloody stools. Some types infest by burrowing through the skin, causing skin inflammation.

Infection of people
People can be affected by hookworm penetrating through the skin, especially the feet.

Treatment
Hookworms lay an enormous number of eggs, so the pup's environment can be heavily contaminated. In some places, especially tropical and subtropical areas, you must regularly treat the dog (**as often as every four weeks**) after the first four treatments. Your vet will explain the local situation.

Whipworm

These are called whipworms because they have a long thin front end and a much thicker rear end so that under the microscope they resemble a whip.

Signs

Whipworms bury themselves deep in the gut wall and suck blood. As a result, affected dogs can have anaemia, lethargy, diarrhoea (often dark and tarry looking or containing blood) and sometimes colic.

Treatment

Whipworms are resistant to some of the drugs used to kill round-worm and hookworm. Use a product labelled as being specifically effective against whipworm. Repeat the treatment **as often as every six weeks** in heavily contaminated areas. Also remove droppings from the ground as soon as possible, as these can contain millions of eggs.

Hydatid tapeworm

There are many different types of tapeworm. The most important is the **hydatid** tapeworm, which can be a serious health hazard to people. Occasionally, people can be infected with another type, the dog-flea tapeworm, but it is unlikely to cause serious clinical problems and can be treated easily.

Infection of people

The hydatid tapeworm itself is small (only four to six millimetres long) and has little effect on the host dog. Unfortunately, it has an 'intermediate' stage in its life cycle in which it forms a large cystic structure. If a person picks up hydatid eggs, this can result in large hydatid cysts forming in the abdomen or other parts of his or her body.

Treatment

Fortunately, there are effective treatments to control the hydatid tapeworm in dogs. The main *source* of hydatid infection is through the feeding of raw sheep offal, especially liver, to dogs. If there is *any* possibility of your dog having access to raw offal, or if hydatids are a known problem in your area, treat the dog **every six weeks**.

Other tapeworm

Other tapeworms are larger and more spectacular than the hydatid worm, but they cause relatively few problems for dogs unless there are a lot of them.

Signs
Tapeworms are 'segmented'. They shed the hindmost segments intermittently and these segments contain thousands of eggs. They can be seen in the dog's droppings or around its anus. They are white to yellowish in colour, are mobile when first passed, and resemble an elongated barrel or a cucumber seed.

The most common tapeworm shares its life cycle with the dog flea. Hence, control of fleas is helpful in the control of this particular worm infestation.

What to do with the droppings

Seal the pup's droppings in a bag and dispose of it with the trash. Worm eggs are extremely difficult to destroy. If you leave them in the garden in the pup's droppings, they are likely to re-infect the puppy as well as putting children at risk.

In summary

To be healthy and happy, puppies also need to be worm-free.

Treat all pups for possible worm infestation. Regular worming is essential.

Heartworm

Heartworms are thin, very long worms (as long as a ruler!) that live in the dog's heart and some of the major blood vessels near the heart. Infected dogs can have hundreds of worms living there and clearly, in a heavily infested dog, that heart is not going to work very well.

Heartworm is a problem for dogs in most parts of the world. Even if it doesn't seem like a risk in your area, when you travel with your dog, or if an infected dog moves in nearby, your dog may become infected, so it is best to be on the safe side.

Heartworm is easily prevented and all pups should have routine preventive treatment.

Signs
Only obvious *late* in the course of the condition, signs include a cough, lack of stamina, weight loss, maybe a pot belly and anaemia. By this time the heart may be badly affected. Diagnosis is by blood test and maybe also x-ray and ultrasound.

Source of infection
Heartworm is spread by mosquitoes. Adult heartworms lay an enormous number of their young into the dog's bloodstream. Mosquitoes which then feed on an infested dog will pick up some of these larvae with the blood. The larvae continue developing within the mosquito for about a week and the mosquito will then inject the more developed larvae into the next dog it feeds from.

Infection of people
People and other animals, such as cats, can be infected by heartworm, but it is extremely rare and mainly in individuals with weak immune systems.

Preventive treatment
When the mosquito injects the heartworm larvae into a dog, the larvae actually stay in the body tissues for about five months or more before they have sufficiently developed to

complete their journey to the heart. The aim of preventive treatment is to kill these larvae long before they can reach their target. Begin treatment as soon as the pup is weaned (certainly by twelve weeks, but earlier if possible).

Treatment can be given either **daily** or **monthly**.

Daily These products *all contain the drug Diethyl Carbamazine Citrate or D.E.C.* They are not totally reliable and infection does sometimes occur even in correctly dosed dogs. They are, however, very inexpensive and are available from most pet supply outlets under a variety of trade names.

If the pup is more than six months old you **must not** start on a treatment containing D.E.C. until your dog has been tested and found to be free from infection, as the results could be serious or fatal if the dog already has heartworm.

You must give the drug daily and if you stop for more than two days, for whatever reason, have your dog's blood tested before recommencing dosage.

Monthly A range of products are now available that are extremely safe and very effective. We highly recommend their use. They are available from your vet.

Vaccinate for life!

Vaccination is a simple, effective and (usually) painless way to protect your dog against the most potentially fatal diseases that may threaten it. Vaccines are a fantastic leap forward in medicine.

While we still have great difficulty in treating these diseases once they have developed in the dog, they have become almost rare in many areas. Diseases like distemper, now uncommon, were once the scourge of the canine world. See pages 72-76 for descriptions of these diseases.

AGE	VACCINATE AGAINST	COMMENTS
Around 6 weeks (These are considered 'temporary' vaccines.)	Distemper Hepatitis Kennel cough Parvovirus	The vaccination at this time is not as reliable or long lasting as later vaccines. The pup's immune system may not be competent to respond well.
12 weeks	Distemper Hepatitis Kennel cough Parvovirus Leptospirosis Rabies	Certain areas only. Not in Australia, New Zealand or the United Kingdom.
16 weeks	Second Kennel cough Second Parvovirus Second Leptospirosis	Varies with vaccine and breed as to whether this is necessary.

The chart above is a basic guide to timing your pup's vaccinations. Your vet will give you specific advice based partly on the situation and risks in your particular area.

Regular booster vaccinations are *essential* to maintain immunity at effective levels. Your vet will advise you on the timing of these and give you a certificate which has information charting the vaccinations your puppy has received and the due date of forthcoming ones. Most practices will also send you a reminder notice when booster vaccinations are due.

Holidays

What do you do with your pup when holidays come around? It's your responsibility to make suitable arrangements when you are away from home, even if just overnight.

Home care

When you are going to be away for only a day or so, neighbours, friends or family members may be able to look after the pup for you. 'Puppy sitter' services are also available in many areas (a puppy sitter will come into your home to walk and feed your pup).

Puppies don't always fit in with your travel plans.

Puppies quickly become bored and lonely when left alone and are liable to get into trouble. Some will make extremely determined efforts to escape, so your defences must be tight. Obviously, a pup that has escaped is in great danger of becoming lost or even injured or killed.

It is your responsibility to make sure the pup has adequate water, food and shelter. You should also ensure it is given sufficient exercise by its temporary carer.

An unhappy pup may whine or bark and is likely to upset your neighbours, especially if this occurs at night. This can be minimised if the carer puts the puppy inside somewhere at night and lets it out again the next morning.

In general, home care while you are away is probably not ideal for a puppy.

Very young puppies should not be left unattended for more than a short time.

If you are leaving the pup at home alone, make sure the area is escape proof.

Boarding

Boarding kennels are set up specifically to meet all the needs of your dog while you are away. They vary in the quality of care given and the attitude of the workers, so ask your friends or vet for specific recommendations. You may even want to visit a few on your short list.

What to look for

Look for kennels that are clean and well ventilated, and that will allow the dogs plenty of exercise. Ask the owners what the dogs are fed on and if they will cater for special diets. Even if you don't need these extra services, the answers you receive will help you to decide where to leave your puppy. If the kennel will cater for individual puppies, this is a good sign.

What you will need to provide

Owners of a good kennel will ask you to provide a current vaccination certificate and the contact number of a friend and vet. Any medication to be taken by the pup, such as heartworm treatments, should also be provided, clearly labelled with details of when the treatments are due.

Note

If you have a pedigree dog, often your breeder will look after your puppy for you, so this is worth considering.

Travelling with your pup

Most dogs enjoy travelling in the car if they are introduced to it gradually. Frequent stops should be planned so your pup can exercise and have a drink of water. Keep your pup on its lead at these times as a remarkable number of dogs are lost at wayside stops.

Do not allow the pup to roam at will around the car. Many owners fit a grill or mesh that keeps the dog in the rear. Dog harness restraints that fit into seat belts are now available and, although they are rather expensive, they do protect the dog during an accident or sudden stop.

Allow plenty of ventilation, especially on hot days. It is not a good idea to let the dog hang its head out of the window. This can lead to eye and head damage from the impact of insects, dust and grit swept in at high speeds. It is also socially inconsiderate to allow a dog to hang out of the window,

barking at passing dogs and people. But by all means let it sniff the breeze by opening the window a little.

Do not leave your puppy in the car on hot days without water and ventilation. It will quickly dehydrate and die.

Travel sickness
Travel sickness is especially common in young dogs. Fear is partly the cause, although it is primarily a motion sickness which the dog's system will usually adjust to in time. Get your pup used to the car by putting it in even when you are not going anywhere. Then, take it on short trips. If it becomes anxious or upset, don't try to excessively placate it by saying such things as 'it's okay, you'll be okay, you're okay'. This is likely to make the pup even more unsure. Instead, speak to it calmly.

If you must go on a longer journey and the pup is still getting upset, ask your vet for medication that will ease travel sickness. **Do not feed the dog before a long trip.**

Establishing good behaviour

The influence you have over the development of your pup's personality is enormous. In almost every case, there is the potential for a marvellous relationship to develop between you and your dog, but whether it does or not depends largely on you.

Your puppy is learning all the time, not just during 'formal' training sessions to teach it to 'sit' or 'stay'.

The key to establishing a cooperative relationship with your pup is to lay down the basic rules and for everyone in the household to apply them with absolute consistency. This is not hard or cruel. Dogs really appreciate what is clear and simple.

Ultimately, the pup must work out just where it fits into the family hierarchy. Its place should be clearly at the bottom. **You are doing it no favours by making it an equal. In fact this actually causes great stress to the dog.**

Winning the leadership role

Most dogs will try to see what they can get away with and, with varying degrees of enthusiasm, will attempt to take over the leadership role. They do this in canine terms, and you may be

unaware that a challenge is being made until you discover that there are problems with the dog's behaviour. Just feeding the pup at the wrong time or playing the wrong sort of games can lead to trouble. Hard to believe? Read on and you may avoid costly mistakes.

Dominant puppies and how to avoid them

As the pup grows and develops in its first six weeks, it will find a position or rank within its litter. The highest ranking or dominant pup will, by the time it is six weeks old, be the first to feed, will have the best sleeping position and will decide which other pups it will allow to groom it and when. This is not usually achieved through plain fighting and aggression, although there may be a little of that, but more subtly through apparently innocuous games. The pups themselves don't consciously go out to achieve dominance. They are just following natural automatic behaviour patterns. The result nevertheless is that a definite pecking order is established. *The same happens when the pup joins your household.*

Don't create a dominant pup!

All puppies have the potential to become great pets.

When the pup is introduced to a new pack (your family), it has to go through all these little trials and tests again. It is essential that at the end of the contest the pup has not achieved a 'dominant'

status. The dominant dog *will* cause problems. It is not a particularly happy or contented dog in this role, but once it has been achieved, it will take considerable effort to reverse. These are the dogs that growl and snarl at you and may even bite. They are difficult to groom, disobedient and headstrong. They are more likely to be problem barkers and to be untrustworthy with strangers. You really don't want one.

The games pups play (with you!) to achieve dominance

Feeding

The new pup will actually watch to see who eats first in your family. This may be unimportant to us, but not to a dog. The person who eats first is perceived by your puppy to be the leader. In many families, the mother eats last after serving everybody else. As far as the pup is concerned, this means she is of low status.

The pup will try to be fed first. Some are more determined than others, depending on their personality and their ranking within the litter. When food is being prepared, your pup will hang around, maybe whimpering or putting its paws on your legs. The temptation is to assume the pup is hungry (and it probably is!) and feed it. Worse, you may be inclined to give it a titbit from the kitchen bench.

> **Solution** Feeding titbits is not only a very bad habit to get the pup into, as it will come to expect scraps and rewards whenever it makes a suitable fuss, but the pup's interpretation is that it has won food from your possession. If the pup is the potentially dominant type, then the first chink in your armour has been achieved. Don't do it!
>
> Titbits given *outside* as a reward *are* acceptable.

Games

Games are vital to your pup's development and should be a lot of fun for everyone. Pups can be outrageous and funny. They are so exuberant and unrestrained, soft and pliable. They are hard to resist.

Enjoy your pup but be aware that games also help to fashion rank. Be especially careful with dogs that are going to mature at over thirty kilograms

Ball games are natural and fun, but beware the lurking monster.

or with those showing signs of a dominant personality. As with the games people play, these are ways of testing themselves against others. As puppies, they played games with their litter mates to determine ranking. They will do this with you too and you can't afford to make mistakes.

Two good examples are **tug of war** and **chasing a ball**.

Tug of War
This is a simple game that usually starts spontaneously. Your pup may grab at a trailing towel or similar object and give it a speculative pull. You pull back and a contest develops. This is all great fun but there are several things that could go wrong. Firstly, the game may escalate and become serious. The dog will become more and more determined, especially if it has a dominant nature. You may inadvertently increase the stakes by playfully growling at the pup, which will eventually growl back. Some animal behaviour experts claim that *only* dogs who played aggressive games and indulged in this mutual growling will growl at their owners later in life!

Secondly, the person playing usually tires of the game before the dog does and will often just let go of the contested object, allowing the pup to run off shaking and worrying at its prize. This is interpreted by the pup as a win in a contest of strength and will.

Solution *You* may not care if the pup runs off with an old towel or bit of rope, but *it* certainly does. You must *not* let your puppy win. You should usually end up in possession of the object, which you should then put away where the pup cannot get it.

In tug of war or other contests of strength or will, make sure you 'win' in the end most of the time, or don't play at all.

Ball games
Ball games are fun and, for most pups, not much more than that. Some breeds are natural chasers and retrievers. Others can't seem to work out why you keep throwing the ball away. If you want it, why throw it? They just trot off, bemused by your strange behaviour.

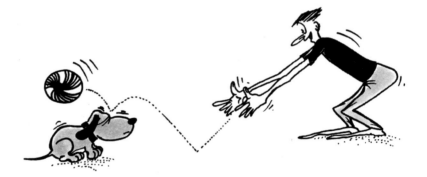

For the dog who does chase and retrieve, whether it's a stick or a ball, it will soon realise that, if it really wants to keep possession, it can. In an open space like a park, a dog is usually quicker and more agile than a person. For dominant dogs, this can lead to the dog having a series of 'wins'.

Solution Don't allow this to happen. By a series of rewards, such as patting and praise, you should ensure that the dog *wants* to give the object back to you when you demand it. Again, this is particularly important with dominant or aggressive dogs. They *will* try you out. Be ready, and don't fall for their game. Train your pup to fetch and to retrieve. You will both be much happier and the dog will be far better adjusted.

Avoid play fighting

Young men and boys often play roughly with their pups. *This can lead to problems*. As adult dogs they are likely to jump up and bite people because they have been handled aggressively as puppies. What started out as a game can easily get out of hand.

Sleeping

You have probably selected a sleeping area for the pup and it will usually accept it at first. At some stage, though, the pup will attempt to take over your sleeping or resting place. Some will be determined and persistent—so be ready.

Eight out ten people are bitten by their dog for the first time when they try to remove it from a bed or chair.

It is commonly thought that when a dog jumps into a chair as the owner gets up, it is for the warmth. It is more likely that the dog is trying to *take over* its owner's preferred sleeping or resting place.

> **Solution** Be firm and consistent. Do not allow dogs to take over any sleeping spot unless you are willing to lose some control. Once the dog has established some hold over a bedroom or chair it can be difficult, or even dangerous, to try to move it.

Grooming

Grooming is an important social activity to dogs. Their sense of touch is well developed. Patting, stroking or even just touching a dog is a potent reward.

As members of a pack, it is the dominant dog who will decide who it will allow to groom it and when. This translates in your situation not only to combing or brushing your dog, but also even to stroking it.

Some dogs will refuse to accept grooming on your terms. They will wriggle and struggle, turn on their backs and generally make it difficult for you. They may run away, or perhaps even growl or bite.

Solution Be firm and insist that the puppy be groomed on your terms. It is not being hurt so don't interpret its resistance as a reaction to pain or discomfort. It is simply challenging your authority. Don't let it get away with this.

Mouthing and biting

All pups investigate new things by sniffing, licking and mouthing them. This is normal and natural. However, if pups are allowed to mouth or even to bite people when they are young, they are likely to go on doing this later. Many owners think this mouthing is cute or just part of being a pup, and therefore allow the pup to get away with it or even encourage it.

Biting is the major reason that dogs have to be euthanased in their first year of life. The time to control this behaviour is when the puppy is very young. Do not wait until it is older. Do not allow or encourage mouthing or biting. Definitely do not indulge in play fighting that includes growling, mouthing and biting.

Pups need to develop their teeth and jaws and are on the look-out for things to chew. They are likely to go through a phase of excessive mouthing and chewing while they are teething. Don't panic too much unless this lasts too long. They are also stimulated by movement and will naturally chase and grab at moving objects such as hands or feet. Some breeds, such as heelers and terriers, are especially prone to this. Excitement, as in games with running, noisy children, will exaggerate this behaviour.

Solution As soon as the pup puts its mouth on a hand or leg say 'no!' and take the hand away altogether or stand still. Waving the hand just out of reach of the pup and wagging an admonishing finger at it only confuses the pup. The moving target is

This is unacceptable. Stop it early.

attractive and tempting and the pup is likely to ignore any command you give it in those circumstances.

If the pup persists, try scruffing it by grasping a big fold of its neck skin just behind its head or by firmly placing your hands around its head. This is very dominant behaviour and is similar to the way the mother would discipline its pups. The pup may squeak or squeal and this can distress some owners. It isn't being hurt—you are simply imprinting correct behaviour

Avoid rewarding the dog for biting or mouthing. You may not mean to do so but if, for example, you take your hand away and then stroke or pat the dog, this may be seen as a reward. It will not discourage the biting.

It may help to give the pup some alternative object to chew—but choose wisely as the pup will believe that this object is okay to chew any time in the future. For example, if you give a shoe, then all shoes may become fair game later. A lump of rope, a nylon bone or rawhide is more suitable.

Dealing with bad behaviour

If your puppy is being difficult and hard to handle, you need to regain control quickly. This can be done using a number of punishments. Two examples are a **rolled up newspaper** and the **'sin**

bin'. Always remember, it is better to reward your dog when it does something right and therefore encourage it, than to have to punish it for misdeeds.

This is dominant behaviour, not just affection.

Rolled up newspaper

You should not hit the pup with your hand, especially around the head.

Hitting will make the pup nervous or fearful and some will learn to respond by snapping at the hand reaching down. If you must use physical punishment, then a *gentle* tap on its rump with a rolled up newspaper is more effective and safer. This does not hurt the pup, but the loud noise gets the message across. Often you only need do this once or twice and then, by simply showing the dog a rolled up paper, slapping it into your palm and saying **'no!'**, you will deliver the same message.

The sin bin

The sin bin is an area in which there is *nothing* that the pup likes—no toys, bedding, food or water. It is an enclosure such as a laundry or toilet where the puppy will be sent if it is naughty.

There is no physical punishment. Instead you are depriving the dog of all it enjoys including company, so it is also important that it cannot see you. It works!

You need only leave the pup in the sin bin for five minutes. When you let it out, do so without any comment at all. Try not to even look at the pup as you release it. It is tempting to say things like 'Now will you be a good girl?' or 'Okay, out you come'. This, however, can be interpreted by the dog as attention and reward and greatly detracts from the effectiveness of the sin bin as a form of punishment.

Overcoming aggression

An aggressive or dominant pup is a real problem. You may be able to reverse or control the situation but you must consider the risks, especially if the pup is a threat to children and to friends. Seek professional advice from your vet or an experienced dog trainer if you are concerned.

If you allow aggressive behaviour to continue, your dog may end up as one of the many euthanased each year.

In some situations, you must part with your dog. Another owner may have more success than you (if your dog is lucky). However, if you recognise the warning signs early or if the dog is amenable to change, you may well be able to achieve a well-balanced, cooperative pet again.

Winning back the leadership role

You must put the puppy back into its place at the bottom of the family hierarchy. Every member of the family must cooperate because unless there is consistency you will fail.

Start your programme by totally—*totally*—ignoring the pup. It is extraordinary how powerful the need for companionship is to a dog. Deprivation of all attention will make your goal achievable in a very short time—from only a few days up to a couple of weeks. The pup's emotional isolation is difficult for some owners

to bear but, if you can steel yourself and do it you will get faster and more certain results.

Your aim is to make the pup feel unwanted for a while. Ignore it. Walk away from it. Do not look at it. Do not speak to it. Food should just be placed down for the pup to find later. After a day or so of this, you can start to give commands. *Only* when the command is obeyed should attention and praise be given, and even then just briefly.

Attaching a long lead

It is useful to attach a long lead to the dog (one or two metres or six to ten feet in length). This may have to be a light chain to avoid it being chewed. It must be worn *right through the day*. With this, you can give a command such as **'Ben, off!'** and, if there is no immediate compliance, you simply get hold of the free end of the lead and pull Ben off. *You* are back in control. Your dog will never work out how to avoid having the lead's end free.

With the long lead dangling, you can control your pup whenever you need to. If, for example, it has taken your slipper, you can bring it to heel immediately. Previously, this would have involved a chase and a confrontation which you might have lost. Similarly, without risk to yourself you can now remove the dog from places it has chosen to hide in or to take over, such as under a table and on your chair or bed. You win every time—you *must*.

At first, leave the long lead on all day and only take it off at night. Only while the lead is on should you pay attention to the pup or reward it with strokes, pats and praise.

This may all seem an unusual way to handle your puppy and it certainly is, compared to the way we discipline people. However, it can be extremely effective in correcting un-acceptable behaviour. Once you have achieved your goal and the pup will now obey you, you must maintain this status quo.

Feeding from now on
Prepare your pup's food at the same time as you make the family meal. Allow it to know the food is there, but do not feed it until after everyone else has eaten. This is a serious lesson for the dog. It is likely to be quite distressed at first and may make great attempts to get you to feed it—perhaps barking or whining or showing similarly agitated behaviour. Don't give in.

Choose a feeding area away from yours. It is probably better to choose a new feeding area so that previous associations are for-gotten.

Take away any uneaten food after five minutes. The pup is to depend on you from now on.

Games from now on
You start the games and *you* finish them, preferably before your dog decides to. If there is any object used in the game, take it and put it away afterwards.

Sleeping from now on
If the pup has previously established its bed in your bedroom or on your bed itself, you should change that situation. In fact, you *must*

if you are to achieve your goal of correcting aggression and/or dominance.

At least it's an old shoe!

You may have to do this gradually. First, move the pup's bedding onto the floor, then to a far corner and eventually outside. Some pups may accept a sudden change, others won't.

Once you have established a new sleeping area for the dog—preferably at a considerable distance away—bar access to your bedroom for ever.

Grooming from now on

If the pup resents being groomed or won't be groomed at all, you must regain control. You choose the time to groom. If necessary, tie the pup up or maybe even muzzle it. Don't let it lie down or roll over to get out of being groomed. Putting it on a table may help.

Speak calmly and evenly as you groom—don't use wheedling or pacifying tones, they only work against you. Don't give in to nuisance behaviour. At the end of a successful session, immediately reward the pup.

In summary, from now on

- Never indulge in wrestling or play fighting with your pup.
- Stop playing games of chase and tug of war.
- Don't give titbits from the hand inside the house.

- Take away any toys or possessions that the dog might guard, even if it has had them since it first arrived.

Obedience work

Training sessions are highly recommended, even if your dog is not a problem. They are effective and enjoyable for both you and your dog. Just a few minutes of obedience training or exercises a day somehow fulfils a basic need in the dog. All behaviour specialists agree that obedience training is extremely useful in overcoming problem behaviour.

The benefits of obedience training are numerous, especially if your pup is showing any signs of excessive independence or rowdiness. It's a sort of therapy. It serves also to improve your control and to reinforce your position as 'boss'.

There are many books available on the subject, but we strongly recommend David Weston's *Dog training: the gentle modern method*.

Diseases

The main diseases we vaccinate against are discussed briefly below.

Distemper

Prior to the development of vaccines, distemper was the major threat to dogs worldwide. It is highly contagious and young puppies are especially at risk.

Signs

The **first stage** starts three to five days after infection and looks a little like a cold. Initially, there is a clear discharge from the pup's nose and eyes which becomes thick and pussy later. The pup will also have a high fever, loss of appetite and maybe a cough.

Most dogs will make an apparent recovery a few days later. Some—not all—then progress on to the **second stage**. This may occur a week or many weeks later.

The second stage is due to an invasion of the nervous system by the distemper virus. Signs vary but may include muscle spasms, twitching or tremors, seizures, loss of balance or limb function, or stupor.

Survivors may be left with permanent nervous conditions such as a muscle twitch, or with other effects such as pitting of the teeth enamel or hardening of the feet pads. There is evidence that the virus can remain in the brain tissue for life and flare up when the dog is old.

Hepatitis (infectious canine hepatitis)

This is a viral disease that causes severe liver damage but it is not transmissible to people. It is highly contagious to other dogs and therefore unvaccinated puppies are at great risk.

Signs

The signs vary with the severity of the infection. In young dogs it may cause sudden death with little warning. More often the puppy gets a high fever, abdominal pain, swollen tonsils, loss of appetite and perhaps jaundice. As a sequel, some dogs develop a cloudy cornea ('blue eye').

The hepatitis infection may persist in a chronic form, resulting in the pup remaining in very poor body condition for the rest of its life.

Transmission

Hepatitis infection can be spread by apparently fully recovered dogs for up to six more months, mainly through their urine.

Kennel cough

The precise definition of kennel cough is somewhat vague. Para influenza virus is the prime cause. One of the bacteria which causes it, *Bordetella bronchiseptica*, is related to the bacteria which causes whooping cough in people. Other bacteria are sometimes implicated and sometimes other conditions causing inflammation of the throat can mimic 'true' kennel cough.

Signs

The pup will develop a deep hacking cough. It may appear as though it has something stuck in the throat, but this is simply thick phlegm that is difficult to dislodge. The dog may become

quite distressed by coughing, but in many cases it can *seem* worse than it really is.

Transmission

Kennel cough is not usually a fatal disease, but is highly contagious. It can be very troublesome where dogs are

living in groups in close proximity to each other, such as at boarding or breeding kennels.

Treatment

The vaccine is usually given against the para influenza virus, but
one can also be given against the *Bordetella* bacteria. An intra-
nasal delivery is used for some kennel cough vaccines, although
most are still given by a subcutaneous injection.

Leptospirosis

There are many forms of leptospirosis. Some affect dogs and people,
others infect other species. In some areas, leptospirosis is common
enough to justify vaccination, especially as it presents a risk to
people. It is not a viral disease, but is caused by a micro-organism
called a 'spirochaete'.

Signs

The signs vary with the type of leptospirosis. The kidneys and
muscles are most commonly targeted, resulting in muscle pain and
fever, listlessness, loss of appetite and perhaps discoloured urine.
In some forms there is liver damage and jaundice, in others diarrhoea, vomiting and mouth ulcers.

Water can be a source of
leptospirosis if polluted by
rats.

Transmission
It is usually transmitted through urine contamination of food or water. Rats or other rodents can be the cause of this.

Treatment
Treatment with antibiotics can be effective, although liver and kidney damage may slow down the overall recovery if the infection has been severe. Vaccination is effective and your vet may recommend it if you live in an area where it is common, or if the pup is likely to be travelling to risky areas or countries.

Parvovirus (canine parvovirus infection)

First seen in 1978, parvovirus infection spread rapidly worldwide, causing epidemics on most continents. Initially, many pups died of heart disease, often with little or no warning. This form of parvovirus is no longer prevalent.

Signs
The major presenting sign now is severe diarrhoea (usually bloody), vomiting, abdominal pain, lethargy, loss of appetite and dehydration. Fatalities are common in young unvaccinated pups.

This virus is very persistent in the environment and is resistant to many disinfectants. It may survive, especially in dog droppings, for up to a year.

Treatment
Treatment can require prolonged hospitalisation with intravenous fluid therapy. Fortunately, the vaccines now available are extremely effective and a sensible vaccination program is your best option.

Rabies

In countries where rabies is present, vaccination against it should be *mandatory*. It is an horrific disease caused by a virus that can infect any warm-blooded animal and can therefore be transmitted to people. It can be fatal for dogs.

Fortunately, rabies is not present in Australia, New Zealand or the United Kingdom. It is present, however, in most other parts of the world including the United States and Canada and most of Europe and Asia.

Signs
The incubation phase of rabies varies. It is usually three to eight weeks but may take up to eight months. The first signs are a slight

fever and a personality change. Previously quiet dogs become irritable and snappy, or perhaps the opposite will happen and aggressive dogs become affectionate. Unfortunately, these signs are not consistent, so never take chances if you have any suspicion at all that you or your animal has been infected by a rabid animal.

As rabies develops, there are two forms it may take:

The 'furious' form

The dog becomes extremely and excessively sensitive to any stimulus and will bite at moving objects if disturbed by lights, noises or even vibrations. As the disease progresses, it may suffer from convulsions, which become more frequent and severe. The dog may die during a convulsion or become paralysed and die.

The 'dumb' form

In this form the virus paralyses the muscles, giving the victim a slack-jawed, hang-dog look. One of the first signs of this form is a change in the dog's bark.

First aid

The aim of first aid is to take immediate action to reduce the impact of an injury until you are able to get professional help. Correct first aid can dramatically improve your dog's chance of survival and reduce discomfort.

Abrasions

An abrasion occurs when the outer layers of the skin are lost but the skin is not completely cut through. It is similar to when we 'skin' a knee or elbow if we slip on gravel.

Treatment
Clean the wound by gently playing water over it or by painting it with a cotton swab soaked in either a *dilute* antiseptic or a mild salt and water solution. Plain, clean water will do. Usually, the

pup will clean the wound by licking it and this is acceptable.

When the abrasion is clean, apply an antiseptic paint or a non-stinging iodine preparation.

Bee and wasp stings

Mostly, these just cause local pain and swelling. Unfortunately, some dogs become hypersensitive to stings and develop a 'whole body' reaction that requires urgent veterinary attention. Only a small percentage of dogs have this reaction. For most dogs, first aid is sufficient.

Treatment

Apply cold to the site if the dog will let you, using ice packs or just cold water. If the paw has been bitten, it might be better to immerse the lower leg in a bucket of ice and water as most dogs are reluctant to let you hold ice onto the paw itself. Pour vinegar over the bite or apply a vinegar soaked pad to the bitten area. This will neutralise the sting.

If the dog is bitten inside the mouth or throat, swelling can make breathing difficult. Given the dog's propensity to chase and snap at noisy moving objects like bees, these cases are surprisingly rare. It is usually just the lips and nasal area that swell up. In most cases, the swelling will go down by itself in two to four hours.

If the dog is having difficulty in breathing, seek veterinary advice.

Bites

Fight wounds and bites from other dogs are common.

Treatment

Infection can easily be prevented if the wound is minor. Clean the area thoroughly, flush with a mild antiseptic solution and apply antiseptic paint or powder.

Deep or multiple wounds need veterinary care. After a dog bite, your dog may have punctures through the skin that carry with them hair, saliva and other bacteria-laden debris. There will be a certain amount of bruising, bleeding and damage to muscle and other tissues. There may not be much to see on the skin surface, but underneath massive infection can build up unless you seek treatment *early*.

Bite wounds that puncture the skin need early veterinary attention.

Bleeding

Dogs have relatively poor circulation of blood to the skin compared with people. They are therefore less likely to experience extensive blood loss from surface cuts and lacerations.

However, cuts to the feet and pads *are* common and they can bleed profusely.

Bright red blood flowing freely or spurting from a wound suggests artery damage. Immediate treatment by the vet is imperative. **Dark blood** which oozes suggests that the damage is less acute.

Pups finds lots of ways to court disaster.

Treatment

Apply firm continuous pressure over the bleeding area or just above it. Most bleeding will then stop within a minute or so. If possible, use a clean pad of cotton gauze but a handkerchief or *damp* cotton will do.

Bandage the pad firmly to the wound using a broad bandage. Be firm but do not apply too tightly or you might cut off the circulation below the bandage.

If blood soaks through the top pad, apply another over it. Do not remove the bottom pad—you will only disturb the clot that is trying to form a seal over the wound.

Long or gaping wounds may need to be stitched by your vet.

Broken bones

Treatment

Do not attempt any splinting. The best dressing is a Robert Jones Bandage (see page 93). This may be worth applying if a vet is not available. To carry a dog with a broken limb, put one hand under the chest and the other just in front of the hind legs, allowing the affected limb to hang free.

Bruises

It is difficult to gauge the extent of bruising on a dog because of its hairy coat. Dogs, unlike people, rarely develop bruises of the skin. Bruising—or bleeding within the tissues—is more likely to occur beneath the skin and involves damage to the muscles, especially next to the bones. This means that there are no visible signs that your dog is bruised except possibly stiffness and soreness in the area. Bruising can be associated with deep injuries and perhaps even severe internal damage.

If the dog has been hit hard, assume bruising, even though you can't actually see it.

Treatment

Ointments, liniments and other treatments designed for bruised people are not suitable for use on dogs. They do little or no good and are liable to damage the dog's skin or irritate its mouth when it tries to lick them off.

For **minor bruising**, the two main remedies are **rest** and **ice**.

Rest
Keep the dog in a quiet and confined area. You may make the bruising worse if you allow excess movement in the first twelve to twenty-four hours. After that, controlled exercise is advisable. Excessive exercise is likely to start the bleeding off again.

Ice
Cool the affected area. Ice itself may not be tolerated by your dog, so try 'cooling wet packs' or even a stream of cold water. Intermittent treatment of a few minutes at a time, repeated several times, will help considerably (especially in the first one to two hours).

Burns and scalds
A **burn** is caused by *dry heat* such as a hot surface or a flame. A **scald** is caused by *hot liquid* such as boiling water or fat. The extent of the damage may be masked by your dog's coat. Extensive burn or scald injury results in acute pain and then shock. Dehydration and severe infections can develop later.

Treatment
Minimise the damage of a burn or scald by reducing the heat. Cool the area immediately by immersing it—or the entire dog if

Cooling down a hot paw.

necessary—in a bath, pool or pond. Alternatively, play a *gentle* stream of water over the area.

Next, soak the area with cold wet cloths. Do not remove the lowermost cloth or you may also pull away damaged skin. Re-soak the cloths frequently and keep this treatment up for five to fifteen minutes.

- **Do not** rub at the wound.
- **Do not** apply ointment, butter or oil to the damaged skin. They will just insulate the skin and prevent the heat from escaping, thus increasing damage.
- **Do not** pull away any dressings that stick to the skin. If you expose the underlying tissue, serious fluid loss and shock may develop faster.

Seek veterinary help for anything more than a very minor burn or scald.

Cane toad poisoning

Dogs usually become poisoned when they bite or pick up a cane toad. The poison is secreted on the toad's skin.

Signs
Initially the poisoned dog will salivate copiously, breath rapidly and have wide open pupils. In severe cases, this progresses to collapse, convulsions and heart failure.

Treatment
Flush the dog's mouth out with water, using a hose if necessary. Seek immediate veterinary attention.

Choking

This occurs if a foreign body such as a large lump of meat, a rubber ball or similar object lodges behind the tongue.

Treatment
Beware! You could easily be bitten if you put your hand in your dog's mouth.

Small dog
Pick your dog up with your hands on either side of its chest and swing it with its *head down* in an arc of 90°. Start with your arms extended in front of you, then swing downwards vigorously, stop-

ping suddenly when the dog's mouth is pointing straight down towards the ground. Repeat until the object is dislodged.

Large dog
Lean over your dog, putting your arms around its chest in a 'bear hug' and give it a sudden hard squeeze. This may help to pop the object out.

Note
In some cases you can chock the mouth open with a block of wood or a cork. Reach in with a long-nosed instrument such as pliers or forceps and try to grasp the object. Even if the dog is unconscious chock the mouth open first before attempting removal.

Cold injury

Frostbite, freezing and hypothermia are not common as dogs are capable of surviving very low temperatures. However, puppies, or dogs that are sick, wet or unable to move (for example after a motor car accident) can be affected.

Signs
It can be difficult to detect cold injury because a dog's skin pallor is not apparent. There may be loss of sensation in the affected area or extremity. The skin will have a blue and fluffy look.

Treatment
Warm the dog *slowly*. A warm bath is excellent. You can also use warm water bottles and blankets and put your dog in a warm, draught-free room. However you decide to do it, warm the dog gradually, using moderate heat only. There may be considerable shivering as the dog recovers and also quite a lot of pain as the circulation returns.

Cuts

Treatment
The treatment of cuts depends very much on the depth and extent of the cut. For all cuts, cover the wound with a pad and apply moderate pressure to stop bleeding. Later, when the bleeding

has stopped, the cut can be cleaned by gently stroking any debris away from the wound using a swab soaked in a *mild* antiseptic solution. Start from the edge of the wound and stroke outwards.

Small cuts will heal quickly. There is usually no need to cover them and most dogs resent bandages anyway. After healing, the wound will contract and scarring is rarely a problem as the coat covers most of it.

Deep, long or extensive cuts will need veterinary attention.

Diarrhoea (See also Vomiting)

In very young pups, even mild diarrhoea should be stopped as they dehydrate quickly. If the dog is still quite bright, is not in obvious pain, is not vomiting and there is no blood in the motion, then home treatment is usually adequate.

Diarrhoea with vomiting can cause rapid dehydration and may be serious. Go to your vet immediately.

Treatment

The aim of treatment is to *rest the puppy's bowel*. Don't give it any food for twelve hours and give it only water to drink (or, preferably, a product that will counter the dehydration and replace lost electrolytes—these are available from your vet or chemist or druggist).

After this time, give it foods that are easily digested and that the pup is used to, in small amounts at a time. Suitable foods include cooked and minced white meats, such as chicken, with some cooked rice, pasta or potato. Unprocessed bran can help to protect the bowel.

Feed the puppy a small amount every few hours. When the diarrhoea is controlled, gradually re-introduce it to its usual diet over two to four days. See advice on feeding milk, page 37.

Drugs useful in the treatment of mild diarrhoea can be obtained from a local chemist or druggist.

Eye injury

Any damage to your puppy's eyes should be taken very seriously. Pups have a tendency to rush into situations without thought for the consequences. Injuries, such as being hit in the eye by a bat while jumping to catch a ball, or getting a face full of irritant pollen from a bush in full flower, are common.

Signs
- Red, inflamed eye.
- Rapid blinking or winking with one eye.

- Dislike of light (hiding away, eyes half closed).
- Very small, or very large pupils.
- One pupil bigger than the other.
- Excessive tear flow.
- Discharge from the eye.
- Swelling, bruising or bleeding of lids.

If only one eye is damaged, it is useful to compare it with the other for the size of the pupil, colour of membranes and so on. Differences usually indicate that something is wrong.

Note

Any blow to the head is likely to affect the eyes, so always have them checked if the pup has suffered a blow on or around the head, even if there is no *apparent* damage.

Treatment

Foreign matter in the eyes, such as dust, pollen, lime, sprays or sand, should be removed, if possible, by flushing the eye with copious amounts of sterile saline. If this is unavailable, clean water will do.

Objects such as grass seeds can often be removed fairly easily if noticed immediately, but they can eventually migrate deep under the lids and you may then require veterinary assistance to remove them. Solid foreign objects, such as bits of glass, may need to be removed under anaesthetic.

Fight injuries

See Bruises, page 80 and Bites, page 78.

Fish hooks

Fish hooks embedded into the lips or swallowed are injuries that are likely to occur if old bait is left on dangling hooks. Pups find them irresistible.

Treatment

If the barb has gone **through the lip**, the hook can be removed by snipping just behind the barb. Where the hook is embedded and/or the dog resists your attempts to help, it is better to calm it and go directly to your vet.

Swallowed hooks rarely cause problems and most pass through its system *unless there is a line attached*. Hooks *with* lines are far more likely to get caught up and act as a 'foreign body'. If the pup is bright and alert, feed it bulky soft foods plus some liquid paraffin and watch its droppings for the fish hook to pass, but seek veterinary assistance if your pup shows the following signs:

- Abdominal pain.
- Is unusually quiet and subdued.
- Lack of appetite.
- Paleness.
- Passing abnormal motions.
- Vomiting.

Fits

Fits or seizures can be frightening to observe. They can be caused if your puppy swallows poisons such as strychnine or snail bait. They can also be brought on by a variety of conditions such as low blood sugar, head injury, liver diseases and so on.

Treatment

While the pup is actually having a fit there is little you can do. **Beware! The seizuring dog is not predictable and may bite, so approach it cautiously.** Holding it tightly may make the seizures worse.

The best you can do is prevent further injury by removing any dangerous objects, like fans, which are near the pup. If the puppy is near a fire, pool or balcony, approach cautiously from behind and drag it away using one hand on the scruff of the neck and one at the tail base or back legs.

Most fits will only last between a few seconds and a few minutes. When the episode finishes, calm your puppy by speaking to it as you would normally. Stroke it gently—but be careful.

If the fit is continuous or repetitive (as in the case of poisoning), get veterinary help as soon as possible. Small dogs can be enveloped in a large blanket to be transported to the surgery.

Head injury

See Eye injury, page 85.

Heat stress

Heat stress is only likely to occur if your puppy is in a confined area such as a car or shed without water or ventilation, or if it is deprived of water for a long period.

Signs

- Panting, becoming rapid.
- Increasing heart rate.
- Gum colour turns bright red, and later to a bluish colour.
- Watery or bloody diarrhoea.
- Eventual collapse and loss of consciousness.

Treatment

Get the dog out of its confinement and cool it by total immersion in cool (not cold) water, or by running a stream of water over it or by using cold soaks. The pup will need plenty of fresh air and cooling.

Seek veterinary attention as complications may occur.

Poisoning

Dogs are inquisitive and indiscriminate about what they eat. Poisoning is relatively common, especially in young pups.

The number of possible poisons is overwhelming. There are so many sources that an entire textbook would be required to cover them all. Only the most common are listed here. If you suspect that your dog has been poisoned it is vital that you take as much information as possible about the suspected substance to your vet. Take the packet, container or whatever. The brand name may not help—it is the ingredients that the vet wants to know about.

If you suspect your dog has been poisoned, contact your vet!

COMMON HOUSEHOLD POISONS

Agent	Sources	Comments
Acids	Battery acids. Some cleaners and polishing agents.	**Do not** induce vomiting. Give milk, milk of magnesia or bicarbonate of soda. If on skin, flush off with lots of water. Take to vet.
Alcohol	Alcoholic drinks. Aftershave. Perfumes. Spirits.	Induce vomiting if conscious. Then give activated charcoal in water. If severe take to vet. This is often due to owner's idiocy.
Alkalis	Cleaners. Solvents Drain cleaner.	**Do not** induce vomiting. Give lemon juice or vinegar or neat evaporated milk. If on skin, flush with lots of water. Take to vet.
Antifreeze	Antifreeze (This has a very attractive taste. Be very cautious.)	**Do not** induce vomiting. Intensive care is needed. Urgently take to vet.
Aspirin	Common household drug. Correct dose 10-15 mg per kg twice daily.	Induce vomiting Can be very toxic in overdose or chronic overuse. May also cause gastric irritation and ulceration.
Barbiturates	Sleeping tablets. Tranquillisers.	Induce vomiting. Keep dog moving about and active. If dog starts to lose consciousness take to vet.
Carbon monoxide	Car exhaust fumes.	Gums turn characteristic cherry red. Fresh air needed urgently—maybe oxygen. Veterinary attention maybe.

Agent	Sources	Comments
Caustic soda	See Alkalis.	
Chlorinated hydrocarbons	Insecticides. (Includes some flea rinses and collars.) Can be absorbed through the skin.	Induce vomiting. Causes excitement, muscle twitching, spasms and tremors. Convulsion or seizure may develop. Exacerbated by handling and light. Wash off excess immediately with soap and water. Take to vet.
Lead	Old paint, especially primer. Linoleum. Batteries. Putty. Some lubricants. Lead sinkers and weights. Solder. Some pipes.	Initially causes diarrhoea, abdominal pain and vomiting. Then, nervous signs which vary from nervousness and hysteria to depression. Can cause blindness, seizures, lack of co-ordination, paralysis. Take to vet.
Metaldehyde (snail bait)	Slug and snail poison. (Very common—dogs are quite attracted to it.)	Induce vomiting. Causes lack of co-ordination, muscle tremors, convulsions. Dog salivates copiously. Induce vomiting if possible. Take to vet.
Organophosphates	Insecticides. (May be ingested or inhaled or absorbed from skin.)	Induce vomiting. Causes muscle tremor, twitching, drooling. Difficulties breathing. Can progress to paralysis and death. Take to vet.
Paracetamol	Type of analgesic. Freely available.	Induce vomiting. Causes liver damage. Onset of signs can take several days. Includes vomiting, diarrhoea, gut pain, depression.

Agent	Sources	Comments
Strychnine (One of the most common maliciously administered poisons.)	Pesticides.	Seizures, convulsions. Highly toxic and potentially lethal. Induce vomiting if possible. Take to vet.
Warfarin	Rat and mouse poisons. Some medications.	Is an anticoagulant. Signs relate to bleeding, but are dependent on where bleeding occurs. There may be small blood spots on the gums, difficulty breathing, weakness, rapid heart rate. Potentially fatal. Induce vomiting. Take to vet.

Plants

The following are *some* of the toxic plants commonly associated with poisoning.

TOXIC PLANTS

Anemone	Delphinium	Larkspur	Rhododendron
Buttercup	Dumb Cane	Lily of the Valley	Russ
Christmas Rose	Foxglove	Mistletoe	Snowdrop
Clematis	Holly	Morning Glory	Sweet Pea
Crocus	Hyacinth	Philodendron	Wisteria
Daphne	Impatiens	Poinsettia	Yew

Treatment

In most cases, dogs will leave poisonous plants alone. If your suspect yours has eaten a possibly poisonous plant, collect samples and, if possible, get a specific identification of the plant. Contact your vet or a Poisons Advisory Centre (see telephone directory).

Treatments vary enormously and are tailored to the specific toxin ingested.

To induce vomiting
- Give half to one teaspoon of **salt** on the back of the dog's tongue or dissolved in water.
- Give one to three teaspoons of **syrup of ipecac** (available at a chemist or druggist).
- Give one to four teaspoons of **hydrogen peroxide** (3 per cent).

Road accidents

Most car accidents result in some bruising and shock. Broken bones, organ damage and soft tissue injury are also common. (See also Bruises.)

Treatment
Beware! Your pup will be in shock and may bite. Approach cautiously and muzzle it if in doubt. Calm it as much as you can. Reassure it, stroke it, soothe it. Any severe bleeding should be treated first by applying pressure directly over or above the wound. See Bleeding, page 78.

    If the pup cannot walk, slide a board or a blanket under it and take it to the vet. It is useful to cover the dog and confine it firmly

Pups are always on the lookout for escape opportunities and don't have much road sense.

(not tightly) on to the board. This prevents excessive movement and stops if from falling or jumping off.

If the pup can walk, help or even carry it to the car and transport it to your vet.

Snake bites

It may be difficult at first to tell if your puppy has been bitten by a snake. In theory, venomous snakes leave twin puncture marks, while non-venomous ones leave a row of punctures. However, these marks are almost impossible to see on a dog's skin.

Signs
- Dilated (wide open) pupils.
- Trembling.
- Salivation.
- May be vomiting.
- Difficulty breathing.
- Red urine (later on).
- Eventual collapse.
Pain at the site of the bite varies with the type of snake.

Treatment
Assume the snake which has bitten your dog is poisonous. The main spread of venom is by diffusion from the bite site. Application of pressure over the wound can save its life. Use a

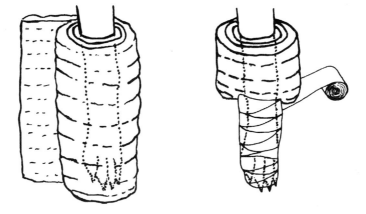

Robert Jones Bandage: Lots of cotton wool or padding—overwrapped with elastic adhesive dressing.

Robert Jones Bandage if you can. Minimise the dog's movement, as movement spreads the poison faster. Carry it if you can.

Do not attempt to suck out poison or to cut into the wound.

Antivenene is available. If you can identify the snake that bit your pup, this may save you a lot of money as the polyvalent antivenene that covers most snake types is extremely expensive.

Spider bites

Just how often dogs are bitten by spiders is debatable. While most spiders are venomous, few can penetrate the dog's skin and coat. The funnel web spider, which is hazardous to people, can bite dogs with very little effect.

Signs
Suspect an insect or spider bite if the dog holds up a paw and shakes it frantically, or paws at its face or mouth.

Treatment
Flush the suspect area with plenty of water then apply ice or cold packs or immerse the area in cool water. Application of a pressure bandage such as a Robert Jones Bandage may help (see page 93).

If the pain persists or there are other signs such as anxiety, muscle spasms, breathing difficulty or lethargy, consult your vet.

Ticks

Some ticks can cause local irritation, dermatitis and sometimes severe blood loss. Others cause paralysis and death. The 'paralysis tick' (found only in certain areas such as the east coast of Australia) is particularly dangerous.

Paralysis tick
Signs
Paralysis will start in your puppy's hindquarters. Your pup will start to drag its toes, then the legs will weaken and will no longer support the body. The paralysis gradually ascends and death occurs from respiratory failure.

A single tick takes three to four days to cause paralysis. Multiple ticks are common, so beware! If you find one tick, keep looking. There may be more.

Treatment
Remove the tick. This can be achieved by levering it up off the skin with forceps or sharp pointed scissors. The aim is to extract the whole tick. Do not squeeze and pull as that will inject more poison into the dog's system. Ticks can sometimes be induced to

let go by inverting a vial of alcohol, turpentine or methylated spirits over them or by painting with nail varnish remover.

An anti-tick venene is available and can be life saving if paralysis has developed.

Vomiting

Vomiting is not a condition in itself. It is part of other diseases and conditions. It can also be a sign of serious illness. However, if the dog is relatively bright and responsive except for the vomiting, simple and sensible home treatment will be enough.

Vomiting is a defensive reflex designed to clear the stomach. If your pup has ingested irritating, noxious or indigestible substances, it is in its best interests to eject it. This is actually to be encouraged, up to a point.

Unfortunately, after a dog has emptied its stomach it may want to drink a lot, then vomit again. The stomach eventually is on something of a hair-trigger. If the dog is allowed to drink too much the vomiting can become serious, as a lot of extra fluids and body salts or electrolytes are lost in persistent vomiting.

Treatment

For **minor vomiting** only (such as travel sickness, over-eating, eating indigestible food, etc).

Withhold all food for twelve to twenty-four hours. For a medium-sized dog allow only half a cup of water to drink every half hour. If necessary, allow the dog to lick at ice blocks covered with a little water.

Introduce food again very gradually. Give only a small amount

of food that is readily digestible such as cooked minced chicken
with a little cooked rice. Go back to normal feeding over three to
five days.

   Seek veterinary attention if :

- The vomiting is persistent.
- There is also profuse diarrhoea.
- There is blood in the vomit.
- The dog is listless or in pain.
- The vomit contains matter which could be poisonous.